Conquering Kudzu

Columbus, OH

Front Cover © Buddy Mays / CORBIS; **3** © Chris Gomersall / Alamy; **4** © PhotoDisc / Getty Images, Inc.; **5** © Adrian Davies / naturepl.com; **6-7** © Jeffrey Lepore / Photo Researchers, Inc.; **10** © Buddy Mays / CORBIS; **12** © Greg Wright / Alamy; **15** © Blaine Harrington III / CORBIS; **Back Cover** © Buddy Mays / CORBIS.

SRAonline.com

An Open Court Curriculum.

Printed in China.

Send all inquiries to this address:
SRA/McGraw-Hill
4400 Easton Commons
Columbus, OH 43219

ISBN: 978-0-07-608823-2
MHID: 0-07-608823-5

1 2 3 4 5 6 7 8 9 NOR 13 12 11 10 09 08 07

The McGraw-Hill Companies

What Are Alien Plants?

Is there an alien living in your neighborhood? There may be! Alien plants are plants that are not native to an area, meaning they do not belong there. A native plant is a plant that still grows in an area where its kind has existed for hundreds of years. Alien plants are not native because they are not growing in their original environment.

Alien plants travel to their new homes in many ways. Migrating birds and wind currents carry seeds hundreds of miles. You might travel to another region and accidentally carry a seed home with you. The seed could grow into an alien plant!

Are Alien Plants a Problem?

Some alien plants do not cause problems. Wheat and oats are alien plants that Europeans brought to America many years ago. Those plants are harmless because they do not spread. They stay where people plant them.

But many alien plants can cause terrible problems. Fast-spreading alien plants are called invasive. Invasive plants grow rapidly, and many of them have lots of seeds, which can produce lots of new plants. New plants can change an area's natural balance. This change can harm soil, animals, native plants, water, and people.

Wheat field

Alien plants

How do some alien plants get out of control? An alien plant often has no natural enemies to stop it from growing. Natural enemies usually keep it in check in its original home. These enemies may include insects, diseases, and weather. In its new home, the alien plant may grow at an alarming pace. Without enemies, the invader can thrive.

As the alien plant grows dense, it will affect habitats, or the places where plants and animals live. Native plants may die because they are crowded out and can't get the sunlight and water they need. Animals that rely on native plants for food may leave the area or starve.

Sometimes alien plants cause erosion when they crowd out native plants. Erosion occurs when water and wind carry away soil. Some native plants control erosion by holding the soil in place. Alien plants do not always control erosion as well as native plants do. When the native plants die, soil needed for growing crops is stripped away. Erosion carries the soil into rivers and streams, where it can pollute drinking water.

Alien plants can carry germs that sicken or kill native plants. Trees become damaged when alien plants strangle them. The trees can even die.

An invasion of alien plants can destroy habitats for native plants and other living things. It can decrease the variety of native animals and plants in an area. Some alien plants produce a lush canopy of leaves. The leaves block light and water that native plants need to survive.

Erosion

How bad is the alien plant problem? Alien plants are one of the greatest dangers to native plants. About two hundred kinds of native plants have become extinct since 1800.

Aliens threaten the U.S. food supply. They invade farms, parks, and forests. Each year, the United States spends billions of dollars fighting alien plants.

Kudzu: The Mighty Vine

Kudzu is an alien plant that has invaded the southern United States. Kudzu is a vine that grows a thick canopy of leaves. This invader thrives in the South.

Kudzu loves the warm weather, plentiful rain, and long growing season of the South. It has no natural enemies there. Kudzu can grow an alarming twelve inches every day in the summer. It covers trees, homes, and power-line poles.

Where did kudzu come from? How did it end up here? In 1876 the United States held a fair in Philadelphia to celebrate the nation's hundredth birthday. Other countries were invited to the fair.

Japanese people brought plants native to Japan, including kudzu. Americans loved the lush plants, with their sweet-smelling flowers. They planted them in their gardens.

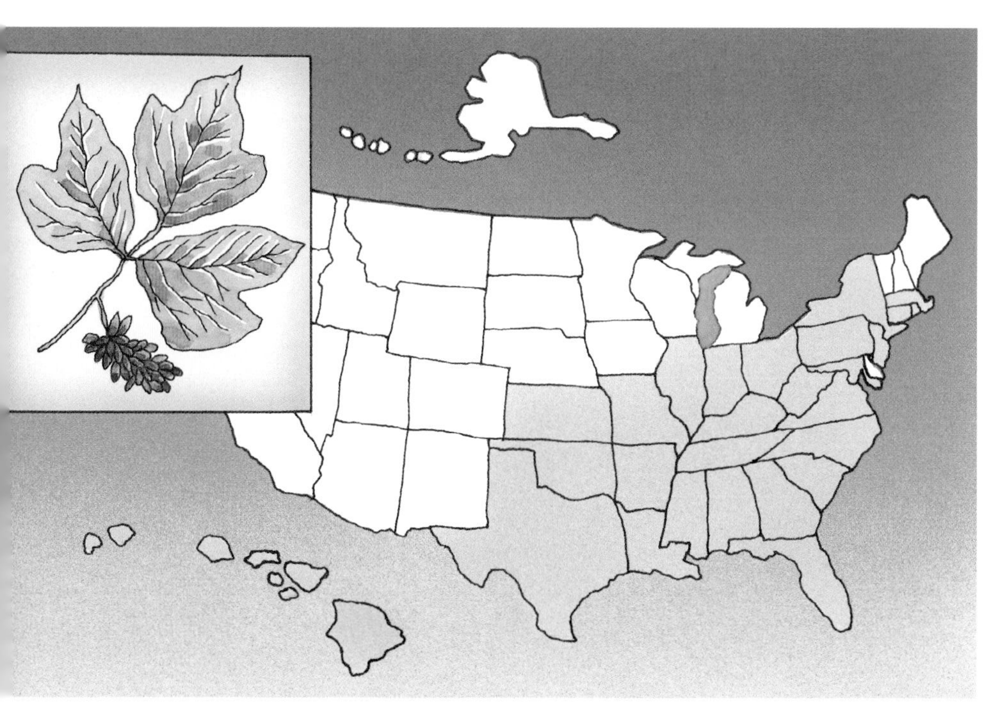

Kudzu in the United States

Soon people began to wonder if there might be other uses for kudzu. In the early 1900s a farmer named Charles Pleas planted kudzu. He noticed that his farm animals loved to eat kudzu leaves. Could kudzu give farmers an endless supply of animal feed? Pleas thought it could.

Pleas told everyone about kudzu. He even sold kudzu through the mail! Before long, many southern farmers were growing kudzu for animal feed.

Trees covered in kudzu

In 1935 people found a new use for kudzu. They believed it could save the South's soil. Planting the land over and over again with crops such as cotton had worn it out. Native plants could not grow. The soil was eroding quickly.

The U.S. government believed kudzu could add nutrients to the soil and keep it from eroding. Workers and farmers planted kudzu in every southern state. But not all farmers liked the idea of planting kudzu. To convince farmers to plant kudzu, the government paid them up to eight dollars an acre to plant it. Farmers planted more than one million acres of kudzu.

Around 1955, Southerners began to look more warily at kudzu. The plant's rapid growth was alarming many people. People in the South began fighting kudzu, but by then it was too late. Kudzu was everywhere.

Today kudzu continues to spread, and it still causes problems for people in the South. There may be as many as seven million acres in the southern United States covered in kudzu.

The dense leaves block sunlight for trees. Whole forests die. Kudzu destroys crops and fruit trees.

Kudzu can damage power lines. Power companies fight it. Road workers remove kudzu from road signs. Railroad workers remove kudzu from train tracks.

Kudzu

Southerners try to kill kudzu by using weed poisons. The weed killer must be sprayed over and over and over. Some kudzu vines must be sprayed for ten years before they die!

In addition, weed poison hurts habitats, killing many plants besides kudzu. People cannot grow new plants in the poisoned area for up to a year.

Many Southerners think about the problem creatively. They can't get rid of kudzu. So why not use it? Craftspeople use kudzu vines to weave baskets. Other Southerners sell kudzu-blossom jelly. People are exploring using kudzu for medicines and even a new kind of fuel.

Stopping Invaders

How can we stop another problem like the kudzu invasion? The best way is to keep invaders from moving into an area. Learning all about problem weeds is a good first step.

Many groups educate people about alien plants. Plant experts help people recognize alien plants. They show people how to stop the new plants from growing.

Cars can spread seeds while moving across the country. Plant experts work with road workers to keep invasive plants from spreading. The experts teach workers to identify alien plants along highways. Then the workers report the weeds or remove them.

Building and logging disturb the ground and can spread seeds. Plant experts help companies make plans for areas where building or logging will take place. The experts remove invasive plants from these areas.

Hikers and campers learn how to avoid areas where alien plants grow. Washing boots before hiking a new trail helps get rid of plants and seeds.

Dogs can pick up plant seeds. Keeping pets on leashes while hiking helps keep seeds from traveling. Hikers should never pick wildflowers they do not recognize. A wildflower might be a weed, and picking it can spread its seeds.

Keeping habitats natural means protecting them from alien plants. Experts ask people to remove alien plants before they spread. They also ask people not to disturb native plants. By following the rules, people can help stop plants from invading.

How can you help with this battle? Become a plant detective! Read books and articles about invasive plants. Learn to identify alien plants in your area and report them. If you don't know if a plant is a problem, ask an expert or a nature organization. Share your knowledge with others. If we join forces, we can all conquer invasive plants.

Vocabulary

thrive (thrīv) (page 5) *v.* To do well.

dense (dens) (page 5) *adj.* Packed closely together; thick.

habitats (hab´ i tatz´) (page 5) *n.* Plural form of **habitat:** The place where an animal or plant naturally lives and grows.

lush (lush) (page 6) *adj.* Thick, rich, and abundant.

canopy (kan´ ə pē) (page 6) *n.* The highest part of a forest where leaves are thickest.

warily (wâr´ ə lē) (page 11) *adv.* Carefully; alertly; cautiously.

alarming (ə lärm´ ing) (page 11) A form of the verb **alarm:** To cause fear.

Comprehension Focus: Classify and Categorize

1. Reread page 4. Into what category can wheat and oats be classified?
2. Reread pages 13 and 14. Classify the information into the category Ways Seeds Can Be Spread.